Choosing the Wide River

By

Chris M. Carmichael

Choosing the Wide River

Chris M. Carmichael

Proexemplar Publishing

ISBN 0-9766736-3-0

ISBN-13 9780976673637

This book is dedicated to all who choose the wide river

Special thanks go to Marie for helpful feedback about this book, and many heartfelt thanks go to all who have offered support on this journey.

With much gratitude to all of my teachers and fellow travelers,

Chris M. Carmichael

Introduction

I put off finishing this short book for over two years. I felt that my life needed to be more together and look perfect before I dared to publish anything resembling self-help. Then one day I realized that this book is not meant to be the final word on anything; rather, it is simply a collection of insights that have been helpful to me on this journey. We are all explorers here. I offer this book with the hope that it may help someone with his or her journey.

Chapter One

Chapter 1

Choosing the Wide River

During a time of loss in my life, I had a dream that felt important. In the dream, I was standing with another woman facing a steep, narrow canal. The canal was fortified with concrete, and the water that sluggishly coursed through the narrow passageway was brown and ugly.

The companion in my dream stood fixated on the unpleasant sight and spoke about how awful it was. As she spoke, I remembered that just a few blocks away the canal turned into a beautiful, wide river. I turned to her, told her about this river, and said I would show it to her. The river was just around the corner -- out of sight, but close by. The woman refused to turn away from the canal and did not believe the river existed.

No matter how I tried to convince her to walk with me so that I could prove to her that the river existed, she would not go with me. She could not imagine that things could be any different from the ugliness she saw before her. I woke from the dream frustrated and sad. The memory of the dream, and the feeling of frustration, stayed with me.

It was obvious, I thought, that the dream was showing me what I already knew -- that sometimes people become stuck in negativity and refuse to listen to other options. Finally, weeks later, another message of the dream hit me. I realized that I was doing the very same thing in my life. When I realized this, I began to see how often I had focused, as if entranced, on the negative side of things.

A negative focus is such an alluring thing, and it can easily become a habit. Sometimes we call it "being realistic" or "facing facts." However, there is a difference between being aware of what *is* and trapping oneself in a cycle of negative focus. When we focus so much on what is wrong, and are caught up in *that*, we remain trapped and blinded to better possibilities.

Stepping aside for a moment to get a different perspective and take positive steps makes a real difference, even if it does not seem so right away. The lesson in this is not just about seeing the glass as half-full, although that is helpful. Rather, this is about making a very conscious decision to pull back far enough to see that you *can* look at things another way.

You can decide to acknowledge the following: just because what you see right this moment appears to be an ugly, polluted canal, if you explore a bit, or you step back far enough, you may indeed see that there is a beautiful wide river just a few blocks away. However, as long as you stay focused on the unpleasantness, and use *that* to guide your behavior, you will suffer. In fact, you may live your entire life without ever seeing the beauty that is just around the corner.

It takes an act of will to turn the eyes away from the negative. It also takes a little courage sometimes and it takes discipline to keep doing it. Most of all, however, actively seeking beauty takes a lot of love for oneself. For many people, that is the hardest part of all.

This is not about choosing the easiest path, nor is it about choosing a difficult path. It is about making a courageous decision to move consciously from an old, limited view to a broader, more open view.

It is about freeing the self and allowing beauty. It is about taking time to appreciate the butterfly that crosses your path, even when you have just lost your job or are in the middle of a divorce. This is not about denial. It is simply about giving more opportunity and attention to all that is beautiful in this world, because what is beautiful in the world deserves more attention.

If there is just one thing I would like you to be able to take away from reading this, it is the following: there are always many options, even if you do not see them right at this moment. Even in the darkest night, you can choose to hold on, knowing that eventually the sun will rise again. You can do this rather than succumb to destructive impulses of the moment. You can ignore the negative impulses and act according to a broader picture.

The fact that you are reading this indicates you seek to feel better, and that you want to make decisions from a clearer place. Whether you have had a career change, have lost a job, or are going through other difficulties, such as relationship strife or a deep loss, right at this moment you can do things that will improve your life.

This takes patience sometimes, but you can do it. It is tempting to feel that things are futile, and you may wonder why you should even bother trying. But, if you do not start, you will not ever get there -- you will not ever get anywhere. Sometimes, it is as if we are sitting in an armchair in the living room and saying, "Gee, I sure wish I could go outside today," while refusing to move. We forget that all we have to do is to stand up and open the door.

So, what has beauty and joy done to us that it deserves to be ignored or even maligned? Why shouldn't we dare to live? Why not open that door and truly, truly live?

Chapter Two

Chapter 2

Let Yourself Off the Hook

One of the cruelest things a person can do is to compare his or her success, or perceived lack of success, with others' success. Making comparisons like this is a sneaky way we make ourselves feel bad. I call it sneaky, because we do not do it on purpose. The conscious mind is usually not aware that we are undermining our own life by envying others' lives.

Most of us have an inner critic. This inner critic has a few different jobs. One of those jobs is to maintain our comfort zone at all cost. It achieves this by finding ways to bring us down whenever we expand beyond our comfortable, safe world. Feeling too happy or content can feel threatening to this inner critic. What better way to squash burgeoning joy than by envying the power, money, beauty or joy that someone else appears to have?

How often do you catch yourself feeling bad about your life because someone else is more popular, wealthy, or happy? Not everyone has this issue, but many do and the sooner it is brought into the light and acknowledged, the better.

There are other reasons we may allow our envious feelings to continue. For some, it is like being a child who wants another child's toy. We secretly believe that if we get upset enough, the universe will give us that toy. It does not really work that way, however, does it? Instead, all we end up with is a bad mood and a feeling of lack.

Since envy is such an incredibly quick and effective way to ruin a good mood, it is a good idea to have tools ready to change it. One way to transform envious feelings into more pleasurable feelings is to use the power of imagination and gratitude.

If you find yourself thinking something like, "My friends are taking a nice vacation while I am stuck here. I never get to go places," you could change your thoughts to, "How nice it is that people I care about have some free time to go and experience joyful things. On behalf of them, I am grateful." When you can say this to yourself without clenching your teeth, you have won half the battle.

At the root of envy is a feeling of lack. Focusing on lack is like focusing on the filthy, narrow canal. If you become too absorbed in the sense of lack, you won't notice the gifts all around you and the gifts that could be waiting for you. Focus on lack long enough and you may never take the steps necessary to receive the gifts waiting for you.

When we stop and turn our attention back to our own lives, and the value and gifts there, we turn our creative energy back to where it belongs and where it will benefit us. When you change your focus away from lack, and towards caring, abundance and appreciation for yourself, you build yourself up, empowering yourself.

Eventually, when envious feelings crop up again, the feelings do not linger so long and feelings that are more positive take envy's place.

Most people claim to want happiness, but frequently choose to put a lot of energy and focus towards unhappy things such as envy. We say we want joy, but do not make the mental shifts necessary for joy.

Why do we sometimes create despair where there need not be despair? Is it an addiction to the rush of emotion? I believe that is the case, sometimes. Perhaps, on a subconscious level, some of us also use negative emotion as a catalyst.

∞○∞

Chapter Three

Chapter 3

Catalysts

When I was young, I wanted to defy gravity. Like many children, when I wasn't jumping off high places, I was experimenting with other ways to fly. One method I tried involved using the garage doors as vertical trampolines. I would take a running start from the end of the driveway and fling myself up against the garage doors. The doors were made of thin wood and had just enough springiness to send me flying. I did this repeatedly to see how long I could stay airborne and how far I could travel.

One day recently, during meditation, that childhood memory kept arising in my mind. Suddenly, it occurred to me that maybe, just maybe, in my adult life I had sometimes placed myself in difficult situations that created tension, or I had kept myself in stressful situations long past the time I could have left, to catapult myself into the next chapter of my life.

It was a shocking discovery. Although I know I was not consciously trying to create hell for myself, and certainly not every bad situation was just a result of my desire for dramatic change, the fact that it happened at all was eye opening. It is healthy and smart to make the best of things and to come out shining despite adversity; it is not healthy or happy-making to hold on to adversity or create it just to force change. Nevertheless, some of us have done this at times.

In any dramatic situation, eventually the tension gets so great that something has to give. Sometimes that tension can feel exciting, even when it is painful (just check out any soap opera on television). Furthermore, the energy that occurs during the release part of the cycle can feel exhilarating. It is a tremendous feeling of relief when we get to the other side of a bad situation --"Whoa, am I glad that is over!"

While this can be an interesting and dramatic way of creating change, it is certainly not the easiest and happiest way of going forward, and living that way is not so much *living* life as it is *reacting* to life.

As I sat there and absorbed the new insights about myself, I knew that, of course, stress and tension is not how I want to welcome or create changes in my life. There are more joyful ways to create change.

Few people consciously invite grief and turmoil into their lives. I want to clarify, as I often do, that I am not at all saying that people ask for bad experiences or that we should look at others and judge them, or that we should tell a suffering person to just get over it. I think it is important and helpful, however, to pay more attention to any underlying feelings or motives we may have regarding our situations.

If you take a deep look at yourself and your life -- and please do it in a loving way --, you may find that you use something or someone as a catalyst. This may not always be a bad thing, but it is something worth paying attention to.

∞∞

Chapter Four

Chapter 4

Please Love Me

Besides using situations or feelings as catalysts, I believe we sometimes hold on to dark moods or negative situations because we fear abandonment from others if we release the mood or situation.

We can become conditioned to believe that we will receive the most love and attention from others when we are feeling poorly or are in bad situations. I suspect that after a while of feeling this way, it can become a habit to dwell in negativity. Eventually, we forget that love is still available when we are happy and whole and not just when we are sad and feeling broken.

Again, it is an unconscious process. I do not think many people sit around thinking, "Oh, I better hold on to this misery so that I will receive affection from people," nor do I mean to imply that people experiencing negative emotion are always seeking attention, or that anyone should ever treat anyone less compassionately.

However, for our own sake, it may be beneficial to notice when we are holding on to a mood or situation out of fear of abandonment. No one wants to think that sometimes we drag out sadness or anger a while on purpose -- but most people do crave connection with others, and I believe much of human behavior arises from the simple feeling, "Please love me."

So, the next time you find yourself in a long-lasting negative state, you could question it and watch how you react to others in that state. If you do find that in a particular situation you are milking a negative emotion, you can step back to find another way of connecting with others. Sadness, grief, anger, and despair all have a time and a place. However, when you feel it is time to embrace other types of feelings, you can do so naturally, and not continue focusing time and energy on old negative feelings out of habit or fear.

This is part of changing an unconscious, fear-based habit, into a healthier and happier way of living and being and is one way to take back a lot of personal power.

∞∞

Chapter Five

Chapter 5

Taking Back More Power

Like many people, I have spent a lot of time and energy angry and resentful towards some people in my life for things they have done. All the anger was justified. Bad things did happen. People do harmful things sometimes. There is no doubt about that.

But, how interesting it is to discover that the anger we let rise up and torment us, long, long after the original events occurred, only punishes us and changes nothing about the past.

It took years before I understood that by allowing myself to keep that anger alive, and allowing stressful energy in each time that I think of some past events, I am destroying moments in the present that I can never, *ever* have back. Each time that I focus on the past and think of all the things I should be angry about, my quality of life in the here and now suffers. By letting my thoughts rehash those experiences, I am continuing a cycle of abuse by abusing myself.

We can change this by turning our attention back to the here and now and finding ways to release old anger. Finding ways to release the anger is not about letting the other person off the hook but has everything to do with letting ourselves off the hook and releasing ourselves from that negative energy bond.

When we feel that familiar pain and anger we always have two choices. We can either feed it or deal with it in other ways. By feeding it, I mean succumbing to those thoughts that may look like, "What a horrible person x was. I cannot believe s/he did that to me. S/he had no right," and dwelling on it, time after time.

Anger affects quality of life in so many ways. It robs us of happy times and harms the physical body. Like all emotions, anger is natural and has a time and a place. There is a difference between experiencing the anger and then letting it go, versus suppressing it or reviving it, however. I don't advocate pretending to yourself or others that you are not angry, for that is just suppression. Suppressing anger is as toxic as dwelling on the anger.

This is not about drawing a happy-face over a gaping wound and ignoring it. It is, instead, about allowing the wound to heal by not picking at it and by nurturing ourselves until it heals.

When we take power back from the past, we are then free to direct it to the present, where it will benefit us, heal us and help us. When we withdraw our energy from those hurtful, situations and avoid picking at them, we can start to heal. When we focus love on to ourselves, we start to heal and we empower ourselves.

∞∞

Chapter Six

Chapter 6

Minding Your Own Business -- how focusing on everyone else but yourself sucks the life out of your life

The more I focus my attention on my life and stop wasting time judging others and worrying about how to "fix" them, the calmer I feel.

Even something as seemingly benign as casual gossip can distract us from our own truth. It doesn't matter if the gossip is about someone we know or a celebrity we have never met; becoming overly focused on another person is a sure way to shut ourselves off from what needs attending in our own life.

Like most things in the world, moderation is important in this. What happens when you spend most of your day worrying about what others are doing right or wrong in their own lives? Where is your energy and attention? When parents think about their children's needs, this is different. However, even parents need time to focus on their own personal growth and needs.

When your focus rests mostly on others' lives, your power is misplaced. When I learned, via some who've gone before me, that it is better and more compassionate to mind my own business before trying to mind everyone else's, that lesson was probably one of the greatest, most compassionate gifts I've ever received.

This doesn't mean I never focus outwardly, and it sure does not mean we should turn a blind eye on suffering and not help one another. However, the next time you notice yourself spending a lot of time mulling over someone else's life at the expense of your own, stop and turn the attention back to your own business, and see how that feels.

After you bring your power back to yourself where it can do the most good, you may find yourself in a much better position to help yourself and others.

∞∞

Chapter Seven

Chapter 7

Compassionate Detachment and Love

Minding your own business can sound so negative. This has to be addressed more fully so that it is not mistaken for coldness towards others. Minding your own business can be done with something called compassionate detachment and there are so many benefits to true compassionate detachment that it bears more mention.

This kind of detachment is not about shutting the heart off from others or not caring what happens to anyone. Rather, it is about caring enough about yourself, and others, to resist the pull of distraction, as I described in the previous chapter, and to resist the pull of negativity.

When someone you know is in a dark place, it is not helpful to that person if you cover your own light to join him or her there. However, we sometimes do this without realizing we are doing it. Feeling sad for someone's suffering is one thing and is a sign of compassion. If we allow that sadness to fill our lives as well, however, and pull our own energy too far down, compassion actually changes into something else.

Imagine going into a friend's house and bringing a lit candle or flashlight because the electricity is off, and you know your friend has no candles or other forms of light. Now also imagine you walk in with your light shining, but instead of allowing it to continue shining, you extinguish it in a misguided attempt to show empathy. What is the result of that? The result is that your friend is no better off; she does not benefit from your light now.

A less metaphorical example is that of speaking to a friend who has been betrayed by someone. In sympathy and compassion, you could simply say something like, "I can imagine that must have really hurt and I am so sorry that happened to you." On the other hand, you could amplify the negative in the world and say, "Yes, people are just awful. The whole world is awful." Then you can join your friend in feeling bad by thinking of how horrible everything is and by focusing on all the cruelty and awfulness in the world. The former way shows empathy but keeps a light shining. The latter way does little but amplify a negative focus.

The darker you allow your mood to become, the worse off you will be and the less able you will be to help your friend, or anyone else, out of a dark space.

A much more serious and complex example is that of trying to help a terminally ill friend. Obviously, this experience will be very difficult, and feeling grief and sadness is normal. Shining your light does not always mean you have to be cheery, when cheeriness is not felt or called for. Shining the light means connecting with what best suits the situation.

In some cases, allowing a friend to see your sadness is appropriate. In other cases, re-focusing on other things is better. The thing to remember is, you cannot die for your terminally ill friend or take on his or her suffering, even if you wish with all your heart that you could. But, I promise you, however your inner truth, your light and love, is expressed -- and truly in a situation like that it is very personal -- you and your friend benefit most if you continue to allow the flow of life and light through you, even as you witness such pain.

A few more points: Compassionate detachment never means laughing at someone's pain or preaching to them to "stop being so negative" when they are suffering.

Compassionate detachment is simply about remaining in your center, and keeping your own energy going strongly, in spite of what may be occurring around you.

Sometimes this can look like the opposite of compassion. However, to stay compassionately detached from another's turmoil enables you to remain shining brightly and the other person will automatically benefit from this.

This is all about recognizing that feeding a monster only makes it stronger. Experiencing another's sadness or despair with compassion is empathy. Drowning in despair for another, on the other hand, only feeds that sadness or despair and is not compassionate.

Forgetting the light within you only amplifies the darkness. Now it claims not just your friend but you as well.

On another important note, compassionate detachment may also be directed towards yourself and the pain within your own life. You can allow yourself to feel whatever emotions you are feeling at any given time without judging yourself for having them and, at the same time, not giving the feelings more fuel to pull you down into despair.

∞∞

Chapter Eight

Chapter 8

A Few Notes on Love

Love is a fascinating, sometimes misunderstood, concept and feeling. We crave it, appreciate it, fear it, revel in it, deny it, forsake it, embrace it and cherish it. But what is IT? So many things seem to fall under the umbrella term, "love." There are certainly many shades of love, many kinds of love, but the love I want to focus on here is the kind of love that is beyond the physical, beyond attachments, beyond the stuff of love songs.

For lack of a better term, I will call this kind of love universal love. It is a flowing energy that underlies many things and it is something that simply is. This kind of love has the advantage of permanence, because when something simply IS, it cannot be harmed.

We surround ourselves with noise and it distracts us from the voice within, but we can learn to experience silence, despite the noise surrounding us, and tap into this love. The quiet essence we find inside, I believe, is the voice of love. It is a love like no other for it is a love without conditions.

If I relate to a person because I feel I need them to gratify something in my life or to enhance my sense of self-worth, then I will not relate to the person as they really are but rather as I want them to be to satisfy that need. I will place the person into my own structure, into a box filled with conditions, and my feelings towards them will fluctuate according to whether or not the person behaves as I wish.

Contrary to this, if I relate to a person not out of need but because I see them as they are and want to journey with them, then I am expressing love unconditionally. The ability to do this ties in with our own love towards ourselves.

If I truly love myself, I am not so threatened by the actions of others. I am already complete in myself and do not require others to behave in certain ways towards me in order for me to feel complete. This frees me to connect with others from a place of real love, and not out of need and lack.

This feeling is not always easy to achieve, but I believe that it is a pure and fulfilling type of love that is worth working towards.

Much of what is called love in popular culture seems the opposite of this kind of love. Trying to be someone you are not, or to martyr yourself, to make someone love you, or making a person bend to your will to receive your kindness and affection is not really very loving.

Love is complex. This isn't always black and white. Consider the jaded lover who says, "But I would die for you!" versus the lover who looks lovingly into the eyes and says, "I would die for you." The words are the same but the sentiment can be oh-so-different. In the jaded lover scenario, the words come not from a place of unconditional love. By giving others the ability to influence us to such an extent, we attempt to place a burden, a responsibility on shoulders that are not meant to bear that burden.

Raw neediness sometimes accompanies, or is mistaken for, love. Companionship between two people who take responsibility for their own joy looks much different from companionship between people who are in the relationship -- friendship or partnership-- out of need. It takes inner work to open to a healthier kind of love, but I believe this is also what choosing the wide river is about.

Romantic love is a beautiful thing, but I think beneath the loving gazes and sweet words there must exist this flow of universal, unconditional love or it cannot last. After these few words I want to add that love seems to be a mystery, always exposing a little more of itself as I journey forward. Perhaps the more we open to it, the more it will unveil its true nature to us.

∞∞

Chapter Nine

Chapter 9

Fear

After addressing love, it can be helpful to address an important hindrance to the flow of love -- fear.

Fear is always suspect. I do not mean the fear that arises when you are walking down a dark alley and hear footsteps behind you. That kind of fear is based on survival, and the adrenalin rush produced at those times is necessary to fight or flee a harmful situation.

Most of the time, however, fear is based on ideas rather than reality. Fear easily fuels itself with memories of the past or an imagined, scary future and usually has little to do with the here and now. When you allow fear guide your life, you act from the place of a victim, rather than the creator of your life.

When you decide to let love instead of fear guide your life, however, old parts of the self may arise, saying, "Well, that Pollyanna approach is one great way to make sure you are used and that you make foolish decisions or suffer in other ways." Those parts are mistaking love for naïve weakness.

Letting love guide you does not mean letting others hurt you. It turns out to be quite the opposite. The more love you have for yourself, the quicker you are to leave situations that are not beneficial to you.

Letting love instead of fear guide you means practicing the ability to separate the fearful whisperings in your ear from the truth in your soul. Following the truth in your soul may sometimes mean leaving and other times staying with another person or a situation, but the choice is different because the choice is not based on attachment or fear.

Chapter Ten

Chapter 10

Growing Pains

Written down, the idea of choosing a more positive, open focus in life can sound like it is full of fluffy bunnies, walks in the park, and holding hands beneath the moonlight. My experience so far has been that there is indeed more moonlight, bunnies and walks, because I am less suspicious of them. I now relish with much more fervor each beautiful moment that occurs.

However, the experience is also peppered with resistance from old habits that do not want to die and this can feel disheartening at times. Perhaps for some people one moment of enlightened bliss immediately leads to calm seas. I suspect that for most of us it takes a bit longer for the calm seas to appear.

Moreover, freeing the self from old ties that bind means that life force comes rushing back in to fill that void the stricture's release has left. This can feel overwhelming, for to experience the power of life and love after being numb to these for so long is dizzying and even frightening. Old parts of the self may immediately try to replace those old bindings to retrieve the familiar numbness. It can feel like a battle, but I believe that you can win it if you really wish to and hang on through the bumpy ride.

You may also experience moments of surprise. Some resistance/bindings people carry around have been there so long that these go unnoticed until they fall away.

Another aspect of growing pains involves other people. Friends may feel threatened at the changes they notice in you. This is because humans find something comforting about a person behaving in predictable ways. When the person starts changing before our eyes it can feel uncomfortable, even if the changes are for the better.

How you deal with your friends depends on personal factors, but it is a good idea to remember that suppressing your own truth, covering your own light, benefits no one. If you continue to nurture your own truth, people who are on a similar wavelength will come into your life. Those who are not on that wavelength may leave.

A particularly difficult part of the battle may be your own inner critic who assumes, like some people do, that looking for the beauty in life or having a positive attitude is naïve and silly -- that somehow, people who are like this are less intelligent or less refined than negative people. I will use the following real-life story to help illustrate this.

Years ago, I worked in the shipping area of a factory. The work was often hot and exhausting and morale among employees was low. However, I figured that since I was stuck there for most of the day, every weekday, I would to make the best of it. For my personality type, making the best of things often involves getting a little silly. Light-hearted humor makes the day go by faster for me and helps me release stress.

A co-worker took note of my smiles, my attempts at humor and my general demeanor day after day and finally told me, "Chris, you must have a very stress-free life to smile and crack jokes so much." I could tell she meant it as a jibe, but I don't think she meant it as a serious insult -- she simply dealt with life differently.

The truth was that I was under a great deal of stress at that time. I had experienced many difficult times full of loss and deep grief. I grew more somber for a moment and told her, "There is an awful lot of sadness in life sometimes. Sometimes you gotta laugh so you don't cry. When given the choice between laughter and tears, I try to go for laughter."

I don't mean tears are bad or should be suppressed or that we should ignore real emotions. There is a time to be serious and a time to laugh and joke around. However, since our society sometimes equates a positive attitude with naiveté, we too often hush our laughter and levity and even make up things to gripe about. We do this so that we fit in with others' gripe fests.

Out of habit we will mention things that went wrong -- upon arriving at work we may say, "Oh god, my coffee was cold," (granted, that really can classify as a tragic event) "and then traffic made me want to pull my hair out," yet we will often avoid mentioning the nice things that occurred that morning.

∞∞

Chapter Eleven

Chapter 11

Remembering What Matters Most to Us

In a world where we are often bombarded with problems, real or imagined, how can we maintain a sense of positive direction? Besides actively seeking out mindfulness teachers and like-minded people, one thing that has been helpful to me in the past two years is finding out and remembering what really matters to me.

What is the most important thing for you? I do not mean physical things such as a house, family or money. Rather, what is the soul, the essence, the quality that matters to you? If you find out what that is, you can use that as a guide for estimating how close to your truth you are living. You can then determine more easily if a particular action serves your truth's purpose or does it a disservice. However, do this all without judgment towards yourself.

External accomplishments and conditions:

Most external accomplishments only offer a transient sense of relief or momentary joy. This means that whether we seek the emotional charge from relationships, from career accolades or whatever else, when the thrill wears off and the applause dies down we are left with an empty feeling that begs to be filled again. So goes the cycle and in this cycle we are never really satisfied.

Consider the following statements we may make to ourselves:

If I make this movie, I will be greater/more deserving/better than I am now.

If I write this book, I will be greater/more deserving/better than I am now.

If this person falls in love with me, I will be greater/more deserving/better than I am now.

When we tell ourselves these things, we are giving our self-worth unfair conditions. Our worth, our joy is placed on things outside ourselves. When the relationship fails, what is left then? What is left when all the external falls away is what really matters and what can and should be nurtured, loved, strengthened and appreciated.

When you find out what it is that is truly important to you and what you value within you, then that can act as your reference point with all you do. When we find the sense of okay-ness in ourselves separate from eternal events, this releases us from a cage of conditions -- conditions that must be met before we allow ourselves to feel good. Our actions then become loving endeavors, and not needy endeavors.

∞∞

Chapter Twelve

Chapter 12

Choosing the Wide River *Just Because*

If you choose a positive focus to achieve a particular outcome, temptations may arise if that outcome is not met within a certain amount of time. For example, if you decide today that you will try to focus on positive things because you feel that doing this may bring in more prosperity, what happens if in a month or two you have a financial disaster?

As with all commitments that we place conditions on, when the conditions are not met, or are not met within a certain period, fear and self-doubt have a space to rush in and push us away from that commitment. However, if the decision is made "just because" it is easier to hold to the decision.

There is nothing wrong with having goals. But, to put off living in the present moment and to put off life until the goal is met, or to choose a positive focus only to achieve a future outcome, means that we have missed the point.

The world always changes. As we change, it will change. Choosing to appreciate beauty, to adopt a more positive focus, simply feels better.

Choosing to follow your truth *just because* releases it from conditions. External whims, others' opinions, or your own inner mental chatter and negative conditioning will not as easily sway you. It is the good kind of stubbornness to say you choose it because you choose it. No other reasons are necessary.

Give yourself permission to seek positive feelings and thoughts *just because*. Give yourself permission to take at least as much notice of the beauty in the world as the negative in the world, *just because*. Consider it a gift to yourself, because... *just because* is enough.

∞∞

Chapter Thirteen

Chapter 13

Do Not Ignore the Power of Conditioning

I think we sometimes forget that humans can be easily conditioned. We like to believe we are consciously in charge of all our thoughts and feelings. However, to ignore the effects of conditioning is to ignore a chance for great healing and positive change.

Here is one example of how conditioning can affect a life. When I feel intense joy, the feeling is usually followed by, or intermixed with, fear. Once I became conscious of that fact, I looked at the impact it had on my life. I discovered that I sometimes mitigate pleasure or avoid feelings of intense joy, to avoid the feeling of fear that follows. Alarmed, yet curious, about that, I tried to find out why that would be. Why in the world did joy frighten me?

What I found was that it was partly from conditioning. Several childhood experiences, some traumatic, occurred with or directly after intense joyful experiences. A car accident that just happens to occur at a certain time, or any other traumatic event, can have a big effect, especially on the young, still-developing brain. This, along with what parents or others do or say, plays a part in early conditioning. Someone raised in abusive situations may have a lot of extremely negative conditioning to work through.

The good thing about paying attention to this is we have the power to change our conditioned responses. What you are not consciously aware of, you cannot do anything about. But once you see that, "Aha, this is one reason I hesitate to allow myself feelings of strong joy," for example, you can begin to re-condition yourself. There are many methods that help. The methods are beyond the scope of this book but some examples include hypnotherapy, NLP (Neuro-Linguistic Programming) and EFT (Emotional Freedom Technique).

We can override programming that gets in the way of living life with joy and freedom. We can find energy that is more flowing, develop more compassion for ourselves and discover more peace. When we eliminate old conditioning that blocks us, it becomes easier to choose positive energy to fill our day.

∞∞

Chapter Fourteen

Chapter 14

It Takes Practice and Courage

In the middle of putting finishing touches on this book, the house developed a plumbing leak. I was unable to do anything about the problem as quickly as I wanted to, and this really tested my centeredness. I cursed the leak furiously and developed a really negative attitude about it.

Days later, as I was looking at water damage on the wall and ceiling, I thought of how ugly it was and felt myself become angrier about it. As I continued to look at it, my anger grew and grew until suddenly I remembered the canal in my dream. I realized that there I was, in a similar state of negative focus, and it took days for me to notice what I was doing.

The point of this story is that choosing a new way of being takes practice. In fact, there may never be a time in life when I am always, 100 percent in the present moment and conscious of what I am feeling and allowing. However, I am getting better at recognizing when I am about to spiral into a bad mood or when I am spending far too much time focused on negative things.

I remembered that I have the choice to rant and rave for longer than is necessary. I can get my blood pressure soaring and my adrenalin all worked up over something I have no immediate control over, or I can try to refocus my attention in a more constructive, healthy way.

Life may bring problems, strife, irritation and even tragedies and there is nothing wrong about feeling emotional responses to these things. The point is not to become so stuck in the pain, anger or irritation that the rest of your life suffers. Good feelings deserve equal time.

If you become stuck long enough in a negative space, eventually that negativity becomes the lens through which all is viewed. Joy is placed in the back seat, if it is even noticed at all. Things become so distorted through that lens that finally our natural ability to see or feel beauty is temporarily lost.

Courage

Choosing a new way of being takes practice and emotional courage -- it takes courage to go ahead and do the things you feel are right in your heart and are healthy for you, even when doing so takes you outside your comfort zone.

Fortunately, comfort zones have some give to them. By that, I mean you can change your comfort zone by gradually reaching out to those new experiences you want in your life. It is like stretching the muscles of the body. At first, you may be very stiff and have limited movement. At first, you may not believe you can ever feel happier, calmer or braver. Eventually, with practice, you will discover a broader range of flexibility.

Sometimes we fear this new flexibility and increased range of motion because it seems so foreign, even if we hate the situation we are in at the moment. We sit in our own tight little space and refuse to budge, saying, "This may be limiting me, but it is safe or it is at least something familiar! Who knows what will happen if I reach outside of my walls? Whatever happens, it will mean change and things may be different and I do not know if I really want that!"

Those fears are very normal. Just let them pass on by like a breeze when they come and do not judge yourself harshly for having the fear. Remember that choosing new ways means to allow the possibility that something more positive may be closer than you may realize, but you must first turn your focus away from the negative to see it. Release the fears and release judgment towards yourself for having the fears.

∞◊∞

Chapter Fifteen

Chapter 15

Some Final Words: What Is It You Deserve?

You deserve to experience beauty and joy. You deserve to feel good. You deserve to experience healthy interactions with others. You deserve the right to say "no" to things that feel wrong for your life, and you deserve the freedom to say *yes* to the beauty and joy within you.

Imagine what it would be like to stop placing things in black or white boxes, with no shades of grey. Imagine what it would be like to shed the notion that to be grown up meant strife, pain and losing the ability to play. Imagine what it would be like to relax more and let down your defenses, knowing you are good enough, right here and now, and if you allow your own beautiful spirit to come forth, you will only get better and better.

Imagine how it would be to remember that all people are just people, and being people is good enough, no matter the degree of fame or lack of fame, the wealth or poverty. Imagine seeing past these external trappings and instead relating soul to soul.

Imagine how it would feel to stop comparing yourself to others and acknowledge to yourself your own beauty and worth, right here and now, and celebrate that with great appreciation.

Appreciation for oneself does not have to mean less appreciation for others. In fact, the opposite is true. The more we treat ourselves respectfully and with love, the more we can be with others in a genuine, caring way.

Imagine letting go of the defenses that pretend to protect you, but in truth take so much energy to fortify that they prevent you from experiencing your true self fully on this earth.

The more we choose to value our own worth and the strength within, the more trust we find in ourselves. The more trust we find, the easier it is to create our life from a solid place, instead of in reaction to fear.

Remember that emotions are a powerfully creative force, if directed appropriately. Negative emotion, often renders the opposite of joy, stalling a person's efforts and hiding options behind the veil of anger, sadness, depression, hate or fear. The good news is, if we get a handle on these emotions we can more easily choose where we want to steer our life, despite what appears to be happening all around.

You are a beautiful being in the universe. Nothing said or done in your past changes that fact. Right at this moment, you are fresh and new. Right at this moment, you are as beautiful as you choose to be. It is only a matter of accepting this fact. The choice is always yours. But, no matter the choice you make, you have a light inside of you that shines. It never goes out and is there, and it will continue to be there, whether you wish to acknowledge it or not.

Forgive yourself for those days when you do not see it. Love yourself, always.

∞∞

Chapter Sixteen

Chapter 16

Exercises

Here are a couple of simple exercises to help you connect more easily with love, joy and general acceptance of yourself.

Exercise 1: The Inner Smile.

Sit down comfortably, away from distractions. Close your eyes. Think of a time when you felt tremendous joy. Feel that feeling and hold on to it. If you cannot think of a time in the past, think of something that has not happened yet but that makes you feel joy inside.

Now, let that feeling increase as much as possible, as if you were turning the dial up on a thermostat. Then, let the feeling flow through your entire body. If you feel the urge to smile, go ahead and do so. Direct that feeling to each part of your body, then release and relax by breathing deeply. Stay in that space as long as it feels comfortable. Know that no matter what else happens, you have given yourself the gift of a healing smile at least for a moment. The more you do this, the easier it is to do.

Exercise 2: I Love You.

Sit down comfortably and relax. Feel the feeling of love. If necessary, you can think of a person, pet or place that helps invoke that feeling in you, but the point is the internal feeling and not anything external.

Now, hold that feeling and open to it as much as you can. Do not think about it--feel it. Next, direct the feeling through your physical body. You can start with the head or the toes. It does not matter. Say in your mind (or out loud if that feels better), "I love you," to each part of your body. If you do not mean it at first, do not worry. The mere act of saying it to yourself is enough to start. Make sure to address the whole self, and just repeat to each part, even each cell, "I LOVE YOU". This is particularly healing if done often.

∞∞

About The Author

Chris M. Carmichael writes fiction and non-fiction and enjoys a variety of genres. When she is not busy writing, she enjoys traveling to gain new perspective and meet new people. Chris holds a bachelor's degree in philosophy.